MW00528059

MANIFESTOS FOR THE 21ST CENTURY

SERIES EDITORS: URSULA OWEN AND JUDITH VIDAL-HALL

Free expression is as high on the agenda as it has ever been, though not always for the happiest of reasons. Here, distinguished writers address the issue of censorship in a complex and fragile world where people with widely different cultural habits and beliefs are living in close proximity, where offence is easily taken, and where words, images and behaviour are coming under the closest scrutiny. These books will surprise, clarify and provoke in equal measure.

Index on Censorship is the only international magazine promoting and protecting free expression. A haven for the censored and silenced, it has built an impressive track record since it was founded 35 years ago, publishing some of the finest writers, sharpest analysts and foremost thinkers in the world. In this series with Seagull Books, the focus will be on questions of rights, liberties, tolerance, silencing, censorship and dissent.

THAT'S OFFENSIVE!

criticism, identity, respect

STEFAN COLLINI

LONDON NEW YORK CALCUTTA

Seagull Books 2010

© Stefan Collini 2010

ISBN-13   978 1 9064 9 779 8

British Library Cataloguing-in-Publication Data
A catalogue record for this book is available
from the British Library

Typeset and designed by Seagull Books, Calcutta, India
Printed at Graphic Prints, Calcutta

CONTENTS

'I find that really offensive.'

'Tough. It's not my fault that you have crazy and confused beliefs.'

'You don't understand. This society already treats me like dirt. I don't need some sneering know-all like you making fun of the things I really care about. Not on top of everything else. You ought to show respect for my beliefs, even if you don't agree with them.'

'Respect? Why should I? I think your views stink and I have a right to say so.'

'Well, fuck you!'

'Yeah, and fuck you, too!'

Is that all there is to be said?

* * *

EQUALITY AND RESPECT

Criticism offends. Criticism, in the ordinary colloquial sense of 'fault-finding', seems almost bound to cause hackles to rise and umbrage to be taken, at least on the part of the person or persons criticized. Resentment figures quite largely in the reaction to being criticized, even where—sometimes especially where—there is some acknowledgement of the justice of the criticism. But resentment may also be felt by a third party, made uneasy by a display of judgemental authority and left feeling suspicious of its legitimacy or standing: 'What right have you got to . . . ?'

The structure of this homely everyday version of the experience of being criticized is reproduced when we are dealing with the general public activity of bringing some matter under reasoned or dispassionate scrutiny. Criticism in this sense is not restricted to fault-finding: it may involve a broader analysis of the value or legitimacy of particular claims and practices. Such analysis will frequently be conducted in terms other than those which the proponents of a claim or the devotees of a practice are happy to accept as self-descriptions, and this divergence of descriptive languages then becomes a source of offence in itself. A probing account of, say, the historical and mythical origins of religious beliefs and practices which believers account for in

other, divine, terms may constitute an obvious—but also delicate—example of criticism in this more extended public sense.

If we confine ourselves to the tradi-
tional form of the debate about 'free
speech', it is not difficult for those of a liberal disposition to persuade themselves that
the rights of criticism should be guaranteed
in any tolerably open society, even when the
activity risks giving offence to some of those
being criticized. There will, of course, be
difficult judgements to make in individual
cases, where, for example, the 'offence'
involved is so fundamental or publicly
damaging that it may start to look like a
form of 'harm' from which citizens should
be protected by law. But, broadly speaking,
defenders of free speech have traditionally
seen the issue in terms of a conflict between
power and freedom, or between conventional social attitudes and outspoken truth,
and they have usually not had much

difficulty in deciding in favour of criticism, even where it may give offence.

However, in the early twenty-first century, this question has acquired a new complexity and a new urgency. Those who think of themselves as committed to 'progressive' moral and political causes have come to believe that two of the central requirements of an enlightened global politics are, first, treating all other people with equal respect and, second, trying to avoid words or deeds which threaten to compound existing disadvantages. There tends to be a greater awareness than was the case a couple of generations ago of the indirect ways in which disadvantage is sustained and reinforced. There is greater alertness to the damaging or demeaning effect of the perpetuation of certain negative images or stereotypes of particular groups of (other) people, whether defined by class, disability, gender, race, religion, sexual orientation or something else. There is a stronger initial presumption of equality, granting no special standing or authority to any of those who may be thought to come from the traditionally privileged sections of society or to be occupying roles that once attracted some form of deference. Genuine acceptance of these fundamental principles is signalled by the showing of both consideration and respect to all other human beings, perhaps especially to those who belong to what have been, or continue to be, historically disadvantaged groups. In a fully, and not merely formally, democratic culture, especially one increasingly empowered by successive stages of the electronic revolution, individuals and variously defined social groups are assumed to have an equal right to hold or express their convictions without being 'dissed' by anyone else.

I have written this essay because, while I share the moral and political principles underlying these attitudes, I find myself sceptical about, and at times alarmed by, the conclusions now commonly drawn from them about the topic of 'offence' in relation to the activity of 'criticism'.

In an attempt to clarify what is at stake, this essay addresses the topic in four stages. First, I explore the nature of 'offence', focusing particularly on what might be called the phenomenology or subjective experience of protesting that one is offended. Second, I consider a little more fully what is involved in that kind of reasoned scrutiny of actions or beliefs that we call criticism. Third, I probe contemporary conceptions of 'identity', especially those identities supposedly conferred by belonging to a 'community' within the larger society, whether the community is defined in ethnic, religious or other terms. And finally, I offer a few sketchier thoughts about the kind of world we think we want to live in, looking particularly—and sceptically—at the requirements of 'respect' in our relations with each other. I have deliberately not illustrated my analysis with actual examples drawn from contemporary controversies. Unless presented in properly full detail, such episodes tend to distract rather than illuminate, and I have preferred to concentrate on setting out the logic of my argument in general terms.

In the space available, I can give only a brief exposition of this main argument. So I shall therefore largely ignore two major issues which would, I acknowledge, need to be dealt with more fully in an extended discussion: first, the acceptable legal limits on free speech where matters such as libel, obscenity and public disorder are involved; second, the conceptions of offence and its consequences to be found in the different major world religions. Apart from pressure of space, I plead in extenuation of these

omissions that both topics are more
fully dealt with by other manifestos in
this series.[1]

OFFENCE

Dictionaries can only ever offer snapshots
of the evolving mutations of language use,
but the Oxford English Dictionary may be a
useful place to start. For our purposes here,
we may leave aside that general or legal
sense of offence which means simply all
forms of breaking the law, and concentrate
on the relevant sense, where the Dictionary
entry reads as follows: 'Offence: The act of
offending, wounding the feelings of, or displeasing another; usually viewed as it affects
the person offended.' And the correspon-
ding sense of the verb is defined thus: 'Offend: To hurt or wound the feelings or
susceptibilities of; to be displeasing or dis-
agreeable to; to vex, annoy, displease,
anger; esp. to excite a feeling of personal

annoyance, resentment or disgust in someone.' Even these condensed definitions
suggest two important characteristics of
offence. First, the emphasis is on the subjec-
tivity of the person offended; and second,
offence exists principally in the sphere of
the feelings. Taken together, these two characteristics may suggest that if someone does
not feel offended, then they have not been
offended. And this may in turn seem to entail the reverse proposition, namely that
each individual is the only possible judge
of whether or not they have been offended.

But things are not quite that straight-
forward. Although feelings are central to
the experience of being offended, there is
usually also some element of conviction that
such a reaction is legitimate or justified.
And this reflects the implicit appeal to
some interpersonal standard. It suggests,
in the more important cases, that it is not
simply on account of some odd quirk or

susceptibility of our own that we find ourselves offended. We could in principle demonstrate to a third party why it is not simply that *we* feel offended, and not simply that we *feel* offended, but that the offending act had some objective properties that made this an appropriate response. And this demonstration would involve some appeal to shared values about how people should or should not treat each other.

There is some parallel here with the closely related topic of 'harassment'. Some workplace guidelines about sexual harassment, for example, state that if a person feels that they have been sexually harassed, then sexual harassment has taken place, whatever the intentions of the person or persons accused of doing the alleged harassing. It is easy to see why, in practice, such guidelines may wish to lean in this direction, as a counter to those forms of prejudice or insensitivity that simply do not recognize their unacceptable behaviour as harassment. But since in this matter there may be legal consequences or sanctions against someone accused of sexual harassment, the question of fact cannot be confined to the feelings of the one claiming to be harassed. Some people may be oversensitive; some may be paranoid; and some may be malicious. In itself, the simple claim to have felt harassed cannot quite be enough. In such matters, the law often resorts to the fiction of what a 'reasonable' person would think, though that notion, in turn, may be partly constituted by precisely those widespread assumptions and habits which the guidelines on sexual harassment are attempting to change. In any event, although the feeling of having been harassed is essential to the case, it cannot in itself be sufficient.

There is, in addition, something about the core experience of being offended that makes us pause before endowing the offended person's view of the matter with unchallengeable authority. The dictionary tells us that offending someone involves 'exciting a feeling of personal annoyance, resentment or disgust' in them. But these last three nouns point to a range of notoriously fickle and subjective responses. I may be 'annoyed' by someone's verbal tics or propensity for telling good jokes badly. I may 'resent' the fact that someone is luckier than I am or better endowed with various gifts of nature. I may be 'disgusted' by someone's mere appearance. These feelings are often changeable and usually transient. And, notoriously, no two individuals will find that they react in the same way to the sources of the alleged annoyance, resentment or disgust. How reliably and enduringly can we build on such an unstable base, especially if what we want to build is some set of prohibitions or general guides to conduct?

It is revealing, in this connection, to consider what is implied in the familiar description of someone when we say that he or she 'does not easily take offence'. This is invariably used as a positive description—but why should that be so? The implied contrast is with those who are touchy or prickly, prone to mount their high horses a bit too readily. Perhaps the homely phrase is a reminder that 'offence' is quite a big gun, only to be fired when the situation merits it. Being too ready to find things 'offensive' is a bit like 'crying wolf': it tends to dilute the claim or deprive it of its force. We are most sympathetic to other people's claims about having been offended when we think there was reasonable evidence of the real approach of a wolf.

Consider a representative situation in which a person might claim, in some indignation, 'I find that very offensive.' It might be said, for example, by a woman in response to learning that her male boss had said of her: 'She only got into that row with her colleagues because she was just about to have her period.' What does the response say in such a case? It says that the boss's comment refers, in a presumptuous way, to something not relevant to her professional role; the comment does not take the reasoned case for the woman's side of the original disagreement seriously; it treats her behaviour and her convictions as determined by or at the mercy of one aspect of the state of her body; and it does so as part of a more general prejudice against the rationality of all those who share this property—women of child-bearing age—a prejudice which has historically contributed to the disadvantage and subordination suffered by women in general.

In such a case, the claim to find something offensive says more than that you dislike it or find your feelings hurt by it. It

suggests, first, that your beliefs, not just
your feelings, are intimately involved;
second, that, on the evidence, you do have
a case that others will find appropriate or
persuasive; and, third, that it is about something generally acknowledged to be significant. Moreover, responding with 'I find
that very offensive' is trying not just to dis-
allow a comment but to put the speaker in
the wrong. This is one of the ways in which
it differs from a response such as, 'No, I
don't agree with that explanation for the
following reasons . . .' which neither disal-
lows the comment nor puts the speaker in
the wrong. And for this reason the claim to
find something offensive always risks seem-
ing self-righteous: it raises the moral stakes
and asserts one's own greater moral seri-
ousness. It often suggests that something
the other person has treated lightly or dis-
missively or simply in a conventional way is,
in fact, an area of life that demands greater

attentiveness and an obligation to revise one's habitual attitudes and behaviour.

This is a major reason why claims about offence are now so intimately tied up with beliefs about structural injustice or other historical disadvantage, since efforts to remedy these necessarily entail changes to habitual attitudes and behaviour. At present, in so-called advanced societies, among the chief occasions where something may be condemned as offensive are those when the action or statement in question is alleged to reinforce the subordination of an already subordinated group.

At this point we need to probe a little more closely the phenomenology of the experience of protesting when one finds something offensive. Such a protest involves advancing a claim to a kind of dignity, most often expressed in the current idiom as a demand for 'respect'. Insisting on one's

'equal right to respect' is an attempt to
assert an equality of status on the part of
someone who assumes or fears that he or
she is likely to be denied it. It is a pre-
emptive strategy directed against all those
who may look down on them or put them
down. Something they believe helps to up-
hold such dignity as they are conventionally
accorded seems threatened or demeaned
and, of course, it is those who are vulnerable
or already feel undervalued who have
most reason to be anxious about being demeaned. In practice, therefore, it usually
issues from, or on behalf of, those who
feel themselves to be in some kind of subordinate position, but who claim that their existing perceived disadvantage should not be
compounded by being looked down upon
by those more fortunate. Those in the world
who are rich or powerful or successful or
beautiful rarely demand to be treated with
equal respect—and anyway, equal to whom?

At the heart of the matter is the issue of 'resentment', especially questions about its sources and its legitimacy. The standard definition of resentment is 'a strong feeling of ill-will or anger against the author or authors of a wrong or affront'. As I mentioned earlier, people often feel resentment, in just this sense, in the face of criticism. One ground of such resentment may be the conviction that the criticism in question is simply not true. But the more interesting case is where we, when we're the target of criticism, recognize, at some level, the truth of the criticism and still feel resentful— indeed, feel resentful precisely because we recognize the truth of the criticism. We may, of course, try to justify or buttress our feeling by suggesting that it is unnecessary or inappropriate for the criticism to be made, against *us*, *now*. And more interesting still is resentment against its being made by *them*, perhaps by them of all people. 'What right have they got,' even if what they say is true?

Resentment is, among other things, a
cry of pain. It often expresses some form of
powerlessness: we resent something precisely because, though we don't like it,
there's not much we can do about it. Resentment is characteristically something
that builds up: finding no immediate expression in repressive action, it accumulates
and turns rancid. In some cases, this experience can result simply from being on the receiving end of good arguments. Such
arguments tell us that we are in some way
falling short or in the wrong, and what
makes them doubly enraging is that we see,
or half-see, that they are right. But we also
feel, at the same time, that in not just
meekly acknowledging their truth we are
somehow in the right, too, because we are
standing up for our autonomy. As the
philosopher Bernard Williams observed not
long ago, 'the power of persuasion, however
benignly or rationally exercised, is still a
species of power.'[2] What we rightly call 'the

force of reason' is experienced as a force, and an alien one when it is against us. We are resistant to it, yet we also feel intellectually cornered by it. This state of feeling is fertile breeding ground for rancour.

All this is increased when it is felt that the criticisms compound existing disadvantage. 'I don't need this,' comes the cry, which may be a way of acknowledging that we cannot dispute the truth of the criticisms, only the appropriateness or benefit of their being made now, when we are already vulnerable on other counts. And, in addition, the criticisms may be directed against beliefs, judgements or tastes that are precious to us and which, we may feel, play an important part in defining who we are.

The likelihood of resentment is increased further when the ones making the criticisms are perceived to be already advantaged in certain ways. The tone of voice used, whether metaphorically or

literally, to make the criticisms sounds full
of self-confidence, the self-confidence typi-
cal of those who have long enjoyed the
enefits of certain forms of advantage. Being
criticized by someone who essentially shares
our social or existential plight may be bad
enough, but being criticized by people who
manifestly have it better seems even
worse—it's offensive. What they say may be
true, but that only compounds the offence
of *their* saying it to *us*. Their own relative
good fortune, it is implied, should disqual-
ify them as critics in this case.

As this analysis suggests, it is not always
easy, when considering a claim that something is offensive, to draw a clear line between feelings and beliefs, or between
appealing to shared standards and feeling
cornered by just those standards. Offence
is, therefore, not a wholly subjective matter,
and although the claim to find something
offensive is at present usually seen as an

attempt to prevent some particular line of discussion from being taken any further, it should actually be regarded as initiating a reasoned argument rather than foreclosing on one.

CRITICISM

This takes us back to the question of criticism. To speak of 'reasoned argument' and 'public scrutiny' may at first suggest the staging of set-piece occasions where some action or statement is wheeled before a tribunal of officially appointed guardians of rationality who proceed to deliver judgement. But that would be a very misleading picture of the everyday activity of criticism, not least because criticism is something that all of us do a lot of the time. That is to say, we constantly point to the slippages, implausibilities and non sequiturs in some of the things people say or do, just as we constantly admire or endorse or celebrate

other things they say or do. And we mostly
do this not by setting ourselves up to give
a summary judgement about whether someone or something is 'good' or 'bad', but by
employing the rich resources of our everyday vocabulary, so many elements of which
function as descriptive and evaluative terms
simultaneously. Just as we are constantly understanding and identifying people as
brave, amusing, reliable, inventive or
warm, so we are also constantly finding
people mean, duplicitous, headstrong,
egotistical, dull and so on. We cannot live
without making such characterizations.
In this sense, we are all of us 'critics' much
of the time.

But this is where we start to touch on
some of the most intriguing aspects of the
relations between criticism and offence. For
although we all constantly engage in such
descriptions, there is something about characterizing or 'placing' people in this way

that can seem to diminish them. It may seem to suggest that in possessing the itemized qualities they lack others and so are to be found further down the scale of human limitation than any of us may like to think of ourselves as being. And it can suggest that the ones doing the characterizing take themselves to be regarding these limitations from a higher vantage point—indeed, that it is only because of this relative advantage in elevation that the characteristics can be so clearly discerned and briskly described. The very confidence with which the characterizations are proposed—whether they are thought to be accurate or inaccurate in themselves—may begin to engender resistance, both in those so described and in others witnessing or reading the descriptions. How, it may be asked, can such categorical critical judgements coexist with the fundamental obligation to show others equal respect?

Perhaps we should start by reversing that question and asking: how does respect exist except in the company of critical judgement? To pretend that a mistaken person is not mistaken is not to treat them as one's equal. To consider someone to be too fragile or too touchy or too stupid to bear reasoned disagreement is to condescend to them. Sometimes with young children we let them think their belief is true when it is not because we judge them not yet able to appreciate the reasons or evidence and we don't wish to upset them. But that is precisely not to treat them as equal adults.

Let me be clear: I am not proposing that in subjecting others' actions or views to reasoned scrutiny we ought to aim at giving offence. We are familiar with professional critics, especially perhaps art critics or so-called restaurant critics who try to build a reputation on the basis of calculated outrageousness. That is just some mixture of careerism and arrested development. At a properly serious level, what critics ought to aim at is being just. But justice can be a severe virtue; certainly, it does not always wear a lovable face. Criticism does not kowtow to the feelgoodery of that kind of 'creative writing' circle in which all drafts are wonderful even if some drafts are more wonderful than others. Criticism, in Matthew Arnold's famous and much misunderstood phrase, is 'the endeavour, in all branches of knowledge . . . to see the object as in itself it really is'.[3] And as we know from everyday domestic or intimate transactions, we may most resent those who criticize us or our tastes precisely when we recognize, or half-recognize, that they are right.

We cannot even say categorically that criticism should never mock or make fun of a person or work. Wit is, after all, the expression of perspective, indicating the angle from which something appears as less important than it likes to pretend. Mockery may, in some cases, be an essential means of persuasion, even though it is one that can all too easily backfire. Laughing may be the right response to the emperor's new clothes, and horseplay can be a good way to identify horse shit. Criticism may be irreverent not out of an adolescent desire to cut everything down to size—which too often means not understanding how some things just are much bigger than others—but irreverent in the sense of not taking an individual's, or a book's, estimation of their own significance and gravity for granted.

This might be all very well, it is increasingly observed, if we were just talking about the kinds of disputes that professional critics have among themselves, but now, in 'the real world', much more is at stake—'the real world' being an implausible mythological land invoked by those intent on parading their own greater hard-headedness and lack of naivety. Criticism in the most general sense now threatens, we are commonly told, to damage the values and beliefs which sustain subordinate or minority communities. Criticism threatens to undermine and destroy identity. But does it?

IDENTITY AND CONDESCENSION

We all have a great many identities, and which of them is most relevant in any particular discussion will be a matter of context. Someone may be a woman, heterosexual, middle class, short, a stutterer, a parent, a Labour-voter, an Asian, an accountant, an athlete, an atheist, an Arsenal supporter . . . Some of these 'identities' are, of course, more fundamental than others but not one of them defines this person for all purposes. It is true that in matters where it may seem that the rest of society defines a person in terms of just one of these markers (for example, skin colour)

there is a strong incentive to give priority to
that identity in one's self-definition, though
that may, arguably, be one of the most insidious ways in which prejudice limits
autonomy. But more generally, the defining
error of 'identity politics' is the tendency to
speak as though one characteristic over-
rides all others, thereby homogenizing
those who possess it and imposing a binary
separation from those who do not, but with
whom some members of the designated
group may have far more in common than
they do with fellow-members of their 'own'
group. And this truth about the necessary
plurality of identities also applies to defining someone as a member of a subordinate
group. While it is true that disadvantage is
often cumulative, it remains the case that
individuals who belong to a 'subordinate'
group in one respect may be part of a 'dom-
inant' group in another and much in between. So-called identity is neither wholly

given nor wholly chosen: it is a classification whose reach and usefulness need to be determined according to circumstance.

All this only makes it more important to insist on the following principle: where arguments are concerned—that is, matters that are pursued by means of reasons and evidence—the most important identity we can acknowledge in another person is the identity of being an intelligent reflective human being. This does not mean assuming that people are entirely—or even primarily—rational, and it does not mean assuming that people are, in practice, always and only persuaded by reasons and evidence. It means treating other people as we wish to be treated ourselves in this matter—namely, as potentially capable of understanding the grounds for any action or statement that concerns us. But to so treat them means that, where reasons and evidence are concerned, they cannot be

thought of as primarily defined by being
members of the 'Muslim community' or
'Black community' or 'gay community' or
'cycling community' or any other 'community'. In these familiar phrases, 'community'
is slackly used not just to indicate a group
of people who are assumed to be defined by
having one property in common, but also
to pre-judge the interests they are assumed
to have at stake in the question under discussion. In practice, the people trapped by
each of these huge verbal butterfly nets may
be diverse in many other respects, and
some of these other respects may be much
more important for who they think they are
in relation to most areas of their lives. Attri-
butions of communal identity of this kind,
however affirmative in intention, risk denying to the people so described the opportunity to consider the reasons and evidence
for a particular case on the same terms as
those who do not belong to the community
in question.

But to say this is to recognize that reasons and evidence cannot be internal to one community, even one defined by fundamental religious or political beliefs. Of course, in practice, people starting from different points of view—which may or may not correspond to different social or cultural backgrounds—may differ about what is to count as a 'good reason' or as 'valid evidence', and that difference may not, on any given occasion, be able to be resolved by argument alone. But they cannot begin to articulate that difference of view unless they assume that the other party is, in principle, capable of understanding what each of them would regard as a good reason or valid evidence, which is already to treat them as reflective intelligent individuals not wholly reducible to being members of any one community. This premise is, in fact, being honoured every time someone protests that a particular action or statement is offensive to them,

since such a protest presumes that those to
whom it is addressed can understand, if
only in a limited or confused way, what
would count as illegitimate in the action or
statement being complained of. And indeed, when we say 'if only in a limited or
confused way', we are acknowledging not
just the existence but also the rightful
intellectual or human authority of certain
standards of fullness and clarity. To so 'acknowledge' them—as opposed to simply
asserting them—is to signal that they
cannot just be 'my' or 'our' standards.

And this is also the proper reply to the
fashionable assertion that such arguments
are just the self-serving pieties of Western
liberal elites who mistake their prejudices
for universal truths. In the early twenty-first
century, it is important to insist, against
some well-meaning but confused ideas
about 'tolerance' and 'mutual respect', that
criticism is not exclusively a 'Western' or a

'secular' practice any more than breathing or arithmetic are. Criticism may be less valued or less freely practised in some societies than in others but it is not intrinsically or exclusively associated with one kind of society, in the way that, say, hamburgers or cricket are. And anyway, different cultures are not tightly sealed, radically discontinuous entities: they are porous, overlapping, changing ways of life lived by people with capacities and inclinations that are remarkably similar to those we are familiar with. While there are various ways to show respect for people some of whose beliefs and practices differ from our own, exempting those beliefs and practices from criticism is not one of them.

It might be thought that a diverse, self-consciously plural society would provide a more favourable environment for the free expression of conflicting views than a more homogenous, monocultural society, and in some ways it does. But what we have seen in the last couple of decades— both in the US and in Western Europe—is an increasing trend towards a form of self-censorship on the grounds that coexistence with people who hold fundamentally different convictions requires abstention from the criticism of those convictions. Or, as one commentator put it recently: 'If people are to occupy the same political space without conflict, they have to limit the extent to which they subject each other's deep beliefs to criticism.'[4]

But we should not let this seemingly innocuous sentiment pass without pausing. Its premise seems to be that 'conflict' is the inevitable, and perhaps even justified, outcome of subjecting someone's 'fundamental beliefs' to criticism, where conflict presumably means not just disagreement but actual violence or the threat of such violence. If we do not want such violence to ensue—as, of course, we don't—then, it seems, we must abstain from such criticism. But why, instead of drawing this confused and craven conclusion, do we not suggest that those people whose beliefs are subject to criticism might refrain from violence as a response? Why should it be assumed that the offended are behaving 'naturally', perhaps even legitimately, in expressing their sense of offence through violence, and that it is the critic who is at fault for 'provoking' this violence?

There is a more general assumption at work here which surfaces whenever a book that criticizes, parodies or mocks the cherished convictions of particular groups is withdrawn, or not published in the first place, on the grounds that it constitutes an 'incitement to violence'. The confusion at work here can be exhibited by considering the following contrasting situations. If a leading North London freethinker stands up in front of a howling mob of

secularists—who are already enraged by
Christian criticism of their views about
human reason and autonomy—and urges
them to attack a pair of Christians who are
distributing Bibles to nearby houses, then
this may be seen to constitute incitement to
violence. If a talented Christian author
publishes a book which mocks the latte-
sipping self-assurance of secularists and
which contains scabrous fantasies about
Voltaire's lack of a sexual life, and if that
book is distributed in the usual way by a
large publishing house, then that does not
constitute an incitement to violence. This
latter scenario may, of course, give deep offence to a group which already feels itself to
be in a beleaguered minority in a domi-
nantly—and officially—Christian society.
But if members of that group respond by
engaging in violence then the responsibility
for their actions is entirely theirs. After all,
if, in the course of a debate about deep

beliefs, I suggest that yours are confused in their reasoning and pernicious in their consequences, and you, by way of response, shoot me, we surely do not draw the moral that 'if people are to occupy the same discursive space without resorting to physical violence they have to limit the extent to which they subject each other's deep beliefs to criticism.' Needless to say, there may be situations in which it is prudent to refrain from expressing contentious views, but that does not at all mean that their contentiousness is a legitimate ground for prohibiting their expression in general.

Of course, the rejoinder will quickly come in: life in actual societies does not correspond to some debating club with clear rules of engagement between identically placed speakers. We need to recognize the reality of pervasive structural inequalities between various groups, as well as the insidious power of social conditioning,

the life-destroying impact of economic
exploitation and the multiply corrosive ef-
fects of prejudice. Those at the sharp end
of these forces do not need to have to en-
dure dismissive attacks on the beliefs which
hold their fragile lives together and give
them some sustaining sense of meaning
and belonging.

But, once again, this urge towards pro-
tectiveness may be misplaced and ultimately condescending. A vital part of what
is involved in functioning as a human being
depends on developing the imaginative capacity to see the world through the eyes of
others. If we try to shield a particular group
from experiences that help to develop this
capacity, we risk doing them a profound
disservice. This is, therefore, another reason why we need to defend what playwright
David Edgar has called 'the right to be
offended', the right to hear discomfiting
truths, even sometimes discomfiting lies,

and to have to try to imagine what the world looks like to those who utter them.[5] In this respect, abrogating freedom of expression because the view expressed is offensive may not only deny the rights of the speaker—it may deny the rights of the listener as well.

This argument has a particular bearing on the role of literature and of the arts in general, especially since they have been fertile ground for controversy about offence and censorship in recent decades. One of the ways in which our experience of being human is both extended and defined is through those activities we may broadly classify as 'play'. When we are playing, we suspend or bracket off certain features of reality: we pretend, we allow the imagined to stand in for the actual, and in this way we can get some kind of perspective on the actual, including aspects of it which we are uneasy with or which we can't quite address directly. 'Art' has some resemblance to 'play' in these respects: it's a temporarily roped-off space in which some imagined alternatives to, or modifications of, reality can be explored—can be, as we say, played with. But not everyone likes having his or her life put into that space, however briefly and playfully: 'Bang, bang—you're dead!' 'Don't, that's horrid.' 'Oh come on, I was only playing.' 'Well, some playing isn't very nice.'

Some art isn't very nice either, and the more it seems to comment on our actual lives the less we are inclined to extend to it the equivalent of playground privileges. But acknowledging the special protocols of what goes on in the roped-off area is as important in literature as it is in boxing. Treating an imaginative representation as indistinguishable from the reality it represents—often in rather mysterious ways—puts us in the position of the dog that runs behind the TV screen to catch the rabbit that has just

passed across it. And the upsetting nature
of the representation may be precisely what
makes it a valuable kind of play. Certainly, if
we try to decide for other people what kind
of discomfort they should be spared, we
may find ourselves denying them precisely
the kind of imaginative experience they are
most in need of. Perhaps egotistical old
men shouldn't be forced to watch Shake-
speare's *King Lear*, but nor should they have
the right to prevent it from being staged
because they would find it hurtful. We diminish rather than sustain their autonomy
if we try to second-guess what will offend
their identity in order to protect them.

Even so, it may be said, some beliefs are
just too precious to be played around with.
Classifying something as 'sacred', for example, can be an attempt to put it beyond criticism, at least beyond criticism of other than
a strictly circumscribed kind. The retention
in the UK statute book of the crime of

'blasphemy'—under which certain forms of criticism are held to constitute unacceptably outrageous or profane dealing with the beliefs and rites of the established religion—in effect trades for the same purpose on the residues of a historical situation in which one denomination had a monopoly on such lawmaking. But it is the essence of criticism not to be circumscribed. The fact that some groups of people may claim that they hold certain beliefs at the dictation of an entity they call their 'god' is not a sufficient reason for others to refrain from the critical analysis of those beliefs. And critical analysis is always likely to make appeal to standards of logic and evidence which the holders of the beliefs in question cannot entirely repudiate. This does not mean, needless to say, that such critical discussion is very likely to lead them to change their beliefs; in the short term, it may increase, rather than diminish, antagonism. But it does mean that the believers cannot simply decree that it is impermissible to subject their beliefs to the same kind of scrutiny as is brought to bear on views not designated as sacred. If the criticism turns out to be ill-informed or insensitive, then the believers should point that out as forcefully as they can—that is, they have to engage in the business of giving reasons and citing evidence rather than trying to foreclose the exchange by claiming that it is offensive.

Similar arguments apply to attempts to exempt the views or tastes of any group from reasoned appraisal and measured judgement. However well intentioned, all such attempts are, in the end, condescending. They assume that, in relation to a given topic, those who are in a disadvantaged 'minority' (we are all in minorities in relation to certain topics) need—in addition to efforts to remedy their disadvantage—the further protection of not having their most cherished convictions critically scrutinized. This in effect posits a two-tier society intellectually with the grown-ups deciding not just what may or may not be said in front of the children but who are to count as children in the first place. This eventually engenders a situation in which it is considered acceptable to criticize, mock or give offence to those deemed to be among the privileged but not to those deemed to be among the less privileged—a moral asymmetry which is ultimately corrosive of genuine respect and equality.

Many of the cases in which these principles are involved turn on the question of reinforcing negative stereotypes. It is sometimes argued, for example, that because a work of literature or drama depicts certain categories of people in caricatured or other unflattering ways, it will thereby strengthen the noxious prejudices which other groups in society are alleged to hold about that category, and so that work should be cut or banned. Now, clearly, there can be forms of misrepresentation which, especially in already inflamed circumstances, may be the direct cause of harm to those so misrepresented and there may then be a reasonable case for legal or other intervention. But this is evidently different from cases where the spokespersons for a particular group simply claim that a representation is so much a stereotype that it is offensive. Apart from anything else, these protests tend to underestimate the critical discrimination of audiences where such representations are involved. After all, stereotypes and caricatures have a perfectly legitimate and well-understood role in various kinds of writing and other arts; not all representations attempt to be, or should attempt to be, fully rounded portraits. But readers and audiences know this, and they are

rarely lulled by a stereotype into mistaking
it for the reality. Comedy, above all, trades
in stereotypes, something of which the au-
dience for comedy is usually well aware—
indeed, that is partly what makes them
funny. Just as most forms of censorship are
rendered incoherent by the working premise that other people will be 'corrupted' or
'depraved' by reading or seeing something
even though the censors themselves have
not been, so also there is a similarly patro-
nising assumption in the judgement that
'most people' will not recognize a comic
exaggeration for what (we see) it is.

It is also worth observing that to de-
scribe certain representations in a book
or play as stereotypes is already to engage
in a form of literary criticism. The case
will be made using just those kinds of
characterizations and discriminations
which the protestors may be unwilling to
have applied to their own tastes or beliefs,

including appraisals of fundamental aesthetic or moral worth. This provides a further illustration of the way in which criticism is simply a more focused or sustained version of those forms of identifying, describing and appraising that we do all the time in ordinary life. In this sense, there is no end-state in criticism, no ultimate destination or final resting place. Every act of criticism may itself be characterized, compared and evaluated. The criticism that gives offence may itself be criticized and that criticism replied to in its turn. Protesting that one of these characterizations causes offence is an attempt to interrupt and arrest the endless flux of criticism, to say that there is somewhere it may not go. But however successful it might be temporarily, that objection will in time also be subject to criticism. All attempts to live in a gated community of the mind fail sooner or later.

The confident note struck, deliberately, by that last sentence may in itself make some people uncomfortable. I am well aware that the very briskness and decisiveness of my formulations may engender resistance among some readers, who will take those qualities in my prose to indicate a high-handed disregard for the situatedness and interested character of all arguments. Similarly, my apparent optimism about most people's potential capacities for intelligent discrimination and reasoned argument may strike some readers as wilfully naive, a bland denial of the power of conditioning and prejudice in contemporary societies.

I plead 'not guilty' to both these charges. On the first, it would, of course, have been possible to strike a more hesitant or concessive note, but it seems to me that at the present moment it is important to be unapologetic about repudiating the confused and partial relativism that haunts contemporary discussion of these matters. Arguments are not reducible to the socio-logical markers of those who propound them and all sociological markers are classi-ficatory abstractions, useful for some pur-poses, obstructive for others. On the second charge, I am equally unrepentant. There is plenty of evidence around to suggest that most responses to most issues by most peo-ple most of the time are not the result of a clear-eyed assessment of the reasons and evidence. But even the most hard-bitten observers of that mixture of inherited social prejudice, media-generated hysteria, and badly-calculated selfishness that underlie so much 'public opinion' do not regard their own views—including this hard-bitten analysis—as simply the reflex of social forces outside their control. We all treat ourselves as potentially capable of forming a view based on relevant reasons and evi-dence. My 'optimism' in this essay consists of nothing more than the presumption that, in matters of public debate, we should treat others on the same basis.

AN UNCOMFORTABLE WORLD

The practical upshot of these arguments, I am well aware, may look different in different periods and in different parts of the world. In twenty-first-century London or New York, an outspoken critical essay may result in nothing more damaging than a little *froideur* at the next drinks party. In eighteenth-century France, it might have led the critic to spend some time in the Bastille. In several parts of the world today, publishing their judgements may cost critics their lives. This last outcome is most likely to be the case where offence is given to the possessors of organized power, whether political or religious. Publicly calling tyrants 'tyrants' tends to offend them, and tyrants are never more tyrannical than in the brutal ways they have of dealing with those who offend them. As we know, the crazed will do crazy things, and the crazed are as often to be found wearing the trappings of power as they are the media-caricatured garb of 'the terrorist'. It is too easy to sit in safety and say that brave critics should nonetheless go ahead and publish their criticism: generals comfortably far from the front line are always passionate about the glory of fighting for a good cause. Let me emphasize, therefore, that it is no part of my argument that individuals should wantonly put themselves in danger. Prudence and pragmatism are practical virtues, especially when living in dangerous public circumstances, just as tact or considerateness may properly lead one to hold one's tongue in less threatening domestic settings.

However, in those societies where relatively free public discussion is not just

permitted but is protected by law, we should
resist any temptation to equate offence with
harm. If an action or statement can be
shown to harm someone else, then there is
a prima facie case for considering the use
of legal sanctions to prevent it (only a
'prima facie' case because in many circumstances other considerations may trump
this argument in practice). If an action or
statement merely offends someone else,
there is no such prima facie case. For the
law to be mobilized, the offensiveness has
to be of such a fundamental kind and at-
tended with so many other damaging social
consequences—and that damage demon-
strable to others than those who claim to
suffer from it—that it comes to be counted
as a form of harm. Offending someone's
beliefs, no matter how central they think
those beliefs are to their identity, does not
constitute the kind of harm the law can
rightly be used to prevent.

Of course, it is easy to grant the rights
of free speech to ideas we agree with. The
test of the principle comes in allowing the
expression of ideas that are abhorrent to
us—'so natural to mankind,' as John Stuart
Mill famously put it, 'is intolerance in what
it really cares about.'[6] From the outside, it
may seem fairly obvious where the limits to
free speech lie in a particular society. In a
state that is founded on a lie, where, say,
what is represented as the act of liberation
was really an act of conquest, there may well
be official proscription of certain forms of
historical analysis. Similarly, a theocracy
may not be willing to tolerate anthropologi-
cally informed critical exegeses of its found-
ing texts. In such cases, the constraints on
free speech are imposed from above and
enforced by the use of state power. But
where the inhibition of criticism arises from
genuinely shared convictions, especially
convictions which mark out their holders as

'progressive' and 'liberal' in other ways, then the constraint may be more insidious but even more effective. As the early-nineteenth-century radical journalist William Hazlitt put it: 'The greatest offence against virtue is to speak ill of it.'[7] The truest test of free speech is provided by those forms of expression which offend the contemporary forms of public virtue, above all by appearing, at least on the surface, to infringe equality of respect or to compound the disadvantage of the already disadvantaged.

But it may be that the most humanly significant aspects of this topic are not reducible to the question of what should be allowed and what prohibited. They concern, in a broader way, contrasting visions of what is involved in living an admirable or fulfilling human life. We can perhaps best approach this dimension of the issue by thinking of the contrasting associations of its main terms. When we speak of 'not giving offence', we conjure up a picture of relationships based on considerateness, compassion and solidarity—the opposite of a hard, indifferent, competitive form of society. It is true that we can surround the idea of criticism with associations that are positive in other ways, as I have occasionally done in my choice of vocabulary earlier in this essay: we may speak of it as fearless, outspoken, clear-eyed, discriminating and so on. But we must also recognize the common associations of its being negative, corrosive, destructive, arrogant. I mentioned earlier how being 'just' may be the most admirable quality in a critic but is hardly a lovable one. There is something chilly, impersonal, unyielding about the whole notion of criticism, and there is also the risk of that hardening of the moral arteries that tends to come with the repeated public exercise of judgement.

Moreover, criticism is a tiring business, necessarily involving the making of judgements about matters that can never be susceptible to final or incontestable demonstration. General certainty is not an option any more than is general relativism, which is actually just a disguised form of general certainty. It is not the obvious route to a quiet life. Criticism is always in part about the bringing of another perspective to bear, which is bound to be the perspective of the observer more than the participant, of the critic not the creator. But we are all sometimes participants rather than observers, creators rather than critics and, in these cases, hearing what it looks like to someone else—who may start from a radically different position and who may not cherish what we cherish—can be an uncomfortable experience.

But where, we can ask, does 'comfort' come on any map of a desirable human existence? It seems quite a high priority in everyday life, yet we are always dimly aware that it is at heart a somewhat tame, slippered, unheroic ideal. We may recognize that situations of initial discomfort bring out some of our better and stronger qualities. In a similar way, offence can be like a tonic—nasty to swallow but good for the system. One of Nietzsche's most celebrated aphorisms is: 'What does not destroy me makes me stronger.'[8] As a motto for life, this strikes me as altogether too strenuous and self-improving. There are all kinds of threatening or irritating experiences that we may be better off without, and anyway it is only in retrospect that we can know that a particular challenge has not destroyed us, and it is not obvious that we should be constantly subjecting ourselves to the risk of it turning out otherwise. But as a motto for engagement with criticism, Nietzsche's remark surely does point in the right direction. Having an outsider's perspective trained on our convictions may be an uncomfortable experience, but those of our convictions that survive the scrutiny are likely to be more securely grounded as a result. Indeed, you might even say that if we really care about the things we profess to care about, then we should positively welcome the critical scrutiny of our commitments. We cannot help but be aware that the world is a very uncomfortable, indeed alarming, place; being too comfortable in it may represent a deliberate dulling of our sensibilities, a wilful refusal of engagement. A principled unwillingness to disagree, to criticize, if necessary to offend, may be akin to opting to live in a permanently anaesthetized condition— less pain, certainly, but probably less life too. Whether we would choose it may depend on how strong we were feeling when asked.

These choices and conflicts of value are not wholly resolvable, not even by invoking ideals of social justice. Structural injustice is entrenched in the world in a great variety of unobvious as well as obvious ways. When the feelings and beliefs of those on the receiving end of such injustice are subject to criticism by some of those who are more fortunately placed, resentment is one understandable outcome. In our search for ways of living that do not involve domination and unjustifiable advantage, we are tempted to ennoble the reaction of resentment into an assertion of human dignity, however baffled or intemperate in its expression. Perhaps we should instead try harder to understand the grounds of this resentment, to explore which of these grounds may be justified, and to treat those expressing the resentment as capable in principle of making similar discriminations. The fact that someone feels resentful or offended may be good reason for treating them with compassion or understanding, but it is not a sufficient reason for abstaining from measured criticism of their views.

Similarly, we acknowledge that those who suffer from systematic disadvantage of some kind have a moral claim on those who do not, and that this asymmetry—which often goes along with asymmetries of power of other kinds—provides the prime context in which to address differences of views between them. But at the same time we have to recognize that suffering from some systematic form of disadvantage does not make the sufferers epistemologically privileged. They may, of course, be able to report where the shoe pinches but, overall, their disadvantage does not guarantee them greater insight or command. Indeed, those with a grievance risk becoming defined by the grievance, seeing the world through its prism and having their horizons narrowed instead of expanded. Rather than axiomatically being an indication of complacency or prejudice, relative good fortune may actually be liberating in this sense, enabling the beneficiary to obtain a wider and better-proportioned view. But in neither case are the views reducible to the advantaged or disadvantaged position. They rest on better or worse arguments, and it is the business of criticism to decide which are which. That is always going to involve intellectual procedures that can, in their turn, be contested; beyond certain minimal dictates of logic and inference, there is no indisputably right starting point, no clear-cut criteria of relevance, no limit to what may come to count as evidence. No individual or group gets to rule on these matters, however powerful their political or sociological position. But by the same token, no individual or group can exempt its own reasoning from further scrutiny. And this, needless to say, applies to the views expressed in this essay. The best reward for having dared to venture onto the treacherous terrain of public polemic would be to find that I had provoked others to come up with better arguments. You can at least be sure that I shall not take offence.

My case in this essay is partly an argument against the misuse of otherwise admirable ideals about respect for other people and about not compounding existing disadvantage. It is partly an argument against a confused form of relativism: most forms of relativism are confused, since it would be nearly impossible to live a life as a consistent relativist. It is also partly an argument against the condescension that is involved, despite all appearances to the contrary, in assuming that leaving other people undisturbed in their beliefs—

beliefs which we, but not they, regard as ignorant or confused—should always over-ride giving them the opportunity to recog-nize uncomfortable truths. We want, to put it in the very simplest terms, to live in a world in which people are considerate and supportive of each other, but we also want to live in a world in which we exercise our powers of discrimination and do not flinch from the truth. This may be a conflict from which we cannot escape without at least some loss.

These arguments do not issue in any single policy prescription or code of prac-tice. At most, they touch on some of the assumptions and attitudes we bring to the discussion of policy and behaviour in this area, though that may not be a small thing to do. But they do issue in one important negative injunction, which can be most briefly expressed as follows: when engaged in public argument on matters of ethical or cultural importance, do not be so afraid of giving offence that you allow bad arguments to pass as though they were good ones, and do not allow your proper concern for the vulnerable and disadvantaged to exempt their beliefs and actions from that kind of rational scrutiny to which you realize, in principle, your own beliefs and actions must also be subjected. This is not an exhortation to try to be offensive, though it is an exhortation to be critical— an activity always likely to give offence. But, for others as for ourselves, there are many worse things in life than being offended, and being treated as incapable of engaging in reasoned argument and discrimination is certainly one of them.

Notes

1 See Caspar Melville, *Taking Offence*, and Martin Rowson, *Giving Offence* ('Manifestos for the 21st Century' Series [Ursula Owen and Judith Vidal-Hall eds]) (London, New York, Calcutta: Seagull Books, 2009).

2 Bernard Williams, *Truth and Truthfulness: An Essay in Genealogy* (Princeton: Princeton University Press, 2002), p. 226.

3 Matthew Arnold, 'The Function of Criticism at the Present Time', in *Essays in Criticism* (London: Macmillan, 1869), p. 1.

4 Tariq Modood, quoted in Kenan Malik, 'Kureishi on the Rushdie Affair', *Prospect* 157 (26 April 2009): 28.

5 David Edgar, 'Shouting Fire: From the Nanny State to the Heckler's Veto—The New Censorship and How to Counter It', in *Extreme Speech and Democracy* (Ivan Hare and James Weinstein eds) (Oxford: Oxford University Press, 2009), pp. 583–97.

6 John Stuart Mill, *On Liberty* (London: Longmans, Green and Co., 1867 [1859]), p. 5.

7 William Hazlitt, 'On Cant and Hypocrisy', in *Sketches and Essays* (London: John Templeton, 1839), p. 38.

8 Friedrich Nietzsche, 'Twilight of the Idols', in *The Portable Nietzsche* (Walter Kaufmann ed. and trans.) (London: Penguin, 1976), p. 467.

INDEX
ON CENSORSHIP

Index on Censorship is Britain's leading organization promoting freedom of expression. Our award-winning magazine and website provide a window for original, challenging and intelligent writing on this vital issue around the world. Our international projects in media, arts and education put our philosophy into action.

For information and enquiries go to
www.indexoncensorship.org,
or email enquiries@indexoncensorship.org

To subscribe to Index on Censorship, or find stockists in your area, go to http://www.indexoncensorship.org/getyourcopy
or phone
(+44) 20 7017 5544 for the United Kingdom
or (+1) 518 537 4700 in the United States

www.indexoncensorship.org